SCHOLASTIC

READ & RESPOND

Bringing the best books to life in the classroom

Activities based on *The Amazing Maurice and His Educated Rodents* By Terry Pratchett

Terms and conditions

IMPORTANT – PERMITTED USE AND WARNINGS – READ CAREFULLY BEFORE USING

Copyright in the software contained in this CD-ROM and in its accompanying material belongs to Scholastic Limited. All rights reserved. © 2016 Scholastic Ltd.

Save for these purposes, or as expressly authorised in the accompanying materials, the software may not be copied, reproduced, used, sold, licensed, transferred, exchanged, hired, or exported in whole or in part or in any manner or form without the prior written consent of Scholastic Ltd. Any such unauthorised use or activities are prohibited and may give rise to civil liabilities and criminal prosecutions.

The material contained on this CD-ROM may only be used in the context for which it was intended in *Read & Respond*, and is for use only by the purchaser or purchasing institution that has purchased the book and CD-ROM. Permission to download images is given for purchasers only and not for users from any lending service. Any further use of the material contravenes Scholastic Ltd's copyright and that of other rights holders.

This CD-ROM has been tested for viruses at all stages of its production. However, we recommend that you run virus-checking software on your computer systems at all times. Scholastic Ltd cannot accept any responsibility for any loss, disruption or damage to your data or your computer system that may occur as a result of using either the CD-ROM or the data held on it.

IF YOU ACCEPT THE ABOVE CONDITIONS YOU MAY PROCEED TO USE THE CD-ROM.

Recommended system requirements:
Windows: XP (Service Pack 3), Vista (Service Pack 2), Windows 7 or Windows 8 with 2.33GHz processor
Mac: OS 10.6 to 10.8 with Intel Core™ Duo processor
1GB RAM (recommended)
1024 x 768 Screen resolution
CD-ROM drive (24x speed recommended)
Adobe Reader (version 9 recommended for Mac users)
Broadband internet connections (for installation and updates)

For all technical support queries (including no CD drive), please phone Scholastic Customer Services on 0845 6039091.

Designed using Adobe Indesign
Published by Scholastic Education, an imprint of Scholastic Ltd
Book End, Range Road, Witney, Oxfordshire, OX29 0YD
Registered office: Westfield Road, Southam, Warwickshire CV47 0RA

Printed and bound by Ashford Colour Press
© 2016 Scholastic Ltd
123456789 6789012345

British Library Cataloguing-in-Publication Data
A catalogue record for this book is available from the British Library.
ISBN 978-1407-16056-6

All rights reserved. This book is sold subject to the condition that it shall not, by way of trade or otherwise, be lent, hired out or otherwise circulated without the publisher's prior consent in any form of binding or cover other than that in which it is published and without a similar condition, including this condition, being imposed upon the subsequent purchaser.

No part of this publication may be reproduced, stored in a retrieval system, or transmitted, in any form or by any means, electronic, mechanical, photocopying, recording or otherwise, other than for the purposes described in the lessons in this book, without the prior permission of the publisher. This book remains copyright, although permission is granted to copy pages where indicated for classroom distribution and use only in the school which has purchased the book, or by the teacher who has purchased the book, and in accordance with the CLA licensing agreement. Photocopying permission is given only for purchasers and not for borrowers of books from any lending service.

Extracts from *The National Curriculum in England, English Programme of Study* © Crown Copyright. Reproduced under the terms of the Open Government Licence (OGL). http://www.nationalarchives.gov.uk/doc/open-government-licence/version/3

Due to the nature of the web, we cannot guarantee the content or links of any site mentioned. We strongly recommend that teachers check websites before using them in the classroom.

Author Eileen Jones
Editorial team Rachel Morgan, Jenny Wilcox, Alison Cornwell, Vicky Butt
Series designer Neil Salt
Designer Anna Oliwa
Illustrator Gemma Hastilow
Photo Image of Terry Pratchett: Martyn Goodacre @ Getty Images
Digital development Hannah Barnett, Phil Crothers and MWA Technologies Private Ltd

Acknowledgements
The publishers gratefully acknowledge permission to reproduce the following copyright material:

Random House Group for permission to use the cover for *The Amazing Maurice and His Educated Rodents* written by Terry Prachett. Copyright © Terry and Lyn Prachett, 2001.

Every effort has been made to trace copyright holders for the works reproduced in this book, and the publishers apologise for any inadvertent omissions.

CONTENTS

Introduction	4
Using the CD-ROM	5
Curriculum links	6
About the book and author	8
Guided reading	9
Shared reading	13
Grammar, punctuation & spelling	19
Plot, character & setting	25
Talk about it	32
Get writing	38
Assessment	44

INTRODUCTION

Read & Respond provides teaching ideas related to a specific children's book. The series focuses on best-loved books and brings you ways to use them to engage your class and enthuse them about reading.

The book is divided into different sections:

- **About the book and author:** gives you some background information about the book and the author.
- **Guided reading:** breaks the book down into sections and gives notes for using it with guided reading groups. A bookmark has been provided on page 12 containing comprehension questions. The children can be directed to refer to these as they read.
- **Shared reading:** provides extracts from the children's books with associated notes for focused work. There is also one non-fiction extract that relates to the children's book.
- **Grammar, punctuation & spelling:** provides word-level work related to the children's book so you can teach grammar, punctuation and spelling in context.
- **Plot, character & setting:** contains activity ideas focused on the plot, characters and the setting of the story.
- **Talk about it:** has speaking and listening activities related to the children's book. These activities may be based directly on the children's book or be broadly based on the themes and concepts of the story.
- **Get writing:** provides writing activities related to the children's book. These activities may be based directly on the children's book or be broadly based on the themes and concepts of the story.
- **Assessment:** contains short activities that will help you assess whether the children have understood concepts and curriculum objectives. They are designed to be informal activities to feed into your planning.

The activities follow the same format:

- **Objective:** the objective for the lesson. It will be based upon a curriculum objective, but will often be more specific to the focus being covered.
- **What you need:** a list of resources you need to teach the lesson, including digital resources (printable pages, interactive activities and media resources, see page 5).
- **What to do:** the activity notes.
- **Differentiation:** this is provided where specific and useful differentiation advice can be given to support and/or extend the learning in the activity. Differentiation by providing additional adult support has not been included as this will be at a teacher's discretion based upon specific children's needs and ability, as well as the availability of support.

The activities are numbered for reference within each section and should move through the text sequentially – so you can use the lesson while you are reading the book. Once you have read the book, most of the activities can be used in any order you wish.

USING THE CD-ROM

Below are brief guidance notes for using the CD-ROM. For more detailed information, please click on the '?' button in the top right-hand corner of the screen.

The program contains the following:
- the extract pages from the book
- all of the photocopiable pages from the book
- additional printable pages
- interactive on-screen activities
- media resources.

Getting started

Put the CD-ROM into your CD-ROM drive. If you do not have a CD-ROM drive, phone Scholastic Customer Services on 0845 6039091.

- For Windows users, the install wizard should autorun. If it fails to do so, then navigate to your CD-ROM drive and follow the installation process.
- For Mac users, copy the disk image file to your hard drive. After it has finished copying, double click it to mount the disk image. Navigate to the mounted disk image and run the installer. After installation, the disk image can be unmounted and the DMG can be deleted from the hard drive.
- To install on a network, see the ReadMe file located on the CD-ROM (navigate to your drive).

To complete the installation of the program you need to open the program and click 'Update' in the pop-up. Please note – this CD-ROM is web-enabled and the content will be downloaded from the internet to your hard drive to populate the CD-ROM with the relevant resources. This only needs to be done on first use, after this you will be able to use the CD-ROM without an internet connection. If at any point any content is updated, you will receive another pop-up upon start up when there is an internet connection.

Main menu

The main menu is the first screen that appears. Here you can access: terms and conditions, registration links, how to use the CD-ROM and credits. To access a specific book click on the relevant button (NB only titles installed will be available). You can filter by the drop-down lists if you wish. You can search all resources by clicking 'Search' in the bottom left-hand corner. You can also log in and access favourites that you have bookmarked.

Resources

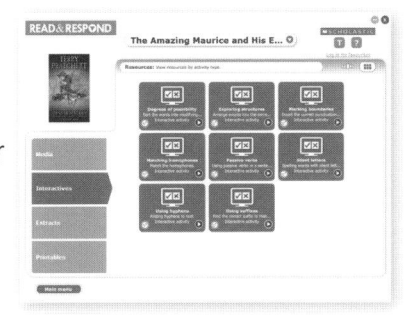

By clicking on a book on the Main menu, you are taken to the resources for that title. The resources are: Media, Interactives, Extracts and Printables. Select the category and then launch a resource by clicking the play button.

Teacher settings

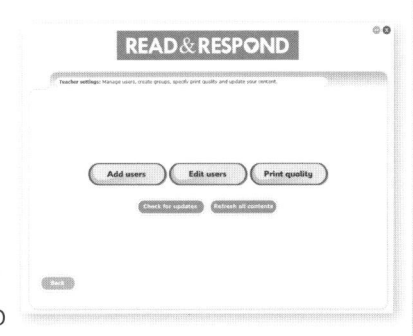

In the top right-hand corner of the screen is a small 'T' icon. This is the teacher settings area. It is password protected, the password is: login. This area will allow you to choose the print quality settings for interactive activities ('Default' or 'Best') and also allow you to check for updates to the program or re-download all content to the disk via 'Refresh all content'. You can also set up user logins so that you can save and access favourites. Once a user is set up, they can enter by clicking the login link underneath the 'T' and '?' buttons.

Search

You can access an all resources search by clicking the search button on the bottom left of the Main menu. You can search for activities by type (using the drop-down filter) or by keyword by typing into the box. You can then assign resources to your favourites area or launch them directly from the search area.

CURRICULUM LINKS

Section	Activity	Curriculum objectives
Guided reading		Comprehension: To draw inferences such as inferring characters' feelings, thoughts and motives from their actions, and justifying inferences with evidence.
Shared reading	1	Comprehension: To draw inferences such as inferring characters' feelings, thoughts and motives from their actions, and justifying inferences with evidence.
	2	Comprehension: To discuss and evaluate how authors use language, including figurative language, considering the impact on the reader.
	3	Comprehension: To check that the book makes sense to them, discussing their understanding and exploring the meaning of words in context.
	4	Comprehension: To distinguish between statements of fact and opinion.
Grammar, punctuation & spelling	1	Composition: To use semi-colons, colons or dashes to mark boundaries between independent clauses.
	2	Composition: To use passive verbs to affect the presentation of information in a sentence.
	3	Transcription: To spell some words with 'silent' letters.
	4	Composition: To use modal verbs or adverbs to indicate degrees of possibility.
	5	Composition: To use commas to clarify meaning or avoid ambiguity in writing.
	6	Transcription: To use further prefixes and suffixes and understand the guidance for adding them.
Plot, character & setting	1	Comprehension: To summarise the main ideas drawn from more than one paragraph, identifying key details that support the main idea.
	2	Comprehension: To predict what might happen from details stated and implied.
	3	Comprehension: To discuss and evaluate how authors use language, including figurative language, considering the impact on the reader.
	4	Comprehension: To draw inferences such as inferring characters' feelings, thoughts and motives from their actions, and justifying inferences with evidence.
	5	Comprehension: To read books that are structured in different ways and reading for a range of purposes.
	6	Comprehension: To identify and discuss themes and conventions in a wide range of writing.
	7	Comprehension: To increase their familiarity with a wide range of books, including modern fiction.
	8	Comprehension: To ask questions to improve their understanding.

CURRICULUM LINKS

Section	Activity	Curriculum objectives
Talk about it	1	Spoken language: To participate in discussions, presentations, performances, role play, improvisations and debates.
	2	Spoken language: To maintain attention and participate actively in collaborative conversations, staying on topic and initiating and responding to comments.
	3	Spoken language: To participate in discussions, presentations, performances, role play, improvisations and debates.
	4	Spoken language: To use spoken language to develop understanding through speculating, hypothesising, imagining and exploring ideas.
	5	Spoken language: To give well-structured descriptions, explanations and narratives for different purposes, including for expressing feelings.
	6	Spoken language: To use spoken language to develop understanding through speculating, hypothesising, imagining and exploring ideas.
Get writing	1	Composition: To draft and write by précising longer passages.
	2	Composition: To identify the audience for and purpose of the writing, selecting the appropriate form and using other similar writing as models for their own.
	3	Composition: To note and develop initial ideas, drawing on reading and research where necessary.
	4	Composition: To draft and write, describing settings, characters and atmosphere and integrating dialogue to convey character and advance the action.
	5	Composition: To select appropriate grammar and vocabulary, understanding how such choices can change and enhance meaning.
	6	Composition: To identify the audience for and purpose of the writing, selecting the appropriate form and using other similar writing as models for their own.
Assessment	1	Composition: To use hyphens to avoid ambiguity.
	2	Transcription: To continue to distinguish between homophones and other words which are often confused.
	3	Comprehension: To draw inferences such as inferring characters' feelings, thoughts and motives from their actions, and justifying inferences with evidence.
	4	Composition: To note and develop initial ideas, drawing on reading and research where necessary.
	5	Comprehension: To check that the book makes sense to them, discussing their understanding and exploring the meaning of words in context.
	6	Comprehension: To identify and discuss themes and conventions in a wide range of writing.

THE AMAZING MAURICE AND HIS EDUCATED RODENTS

About the book

The Amazing Maurice and His Educated Rodents, a children's book in a fantasy series for adults, matches the maturing tastes and literacy curriculum of Upper Juniors. Written by a significant author, it raises issues and dilemmas, and links to a traditional fairy tale.

The main character is Maurice, a streetwise, talking cat. His money-making trick involves a band of rats, clever after feeding on the rubbish dump at the University for Wizards, and a simple boy piper named Keith, paid to lead them away. However, the educated rats question the trick's morality, and Keith fears danger. With different ambitions, they target one final town: Bad Blintz. Keith wants to secure a future playing his flute, the rats need to buy boats to establish an island rat civilization and Maurice plots to abscond with all the money. Bad Blintz proves a poor choice. As the rats infest the town, Maurice and Keith become entangled with a manipulative girl. Trapped, they face powerful dangers: unfamiliar traps and poisons, a rat king, cruel rat-catchers and mind control.

This inventive parody of the 'Pied Piper' tale is funny and fantastic, but also thought-provoking and ethically-challenging. There is humour in the sharp dialogue, inappropriate rat names, and the absurd, story-weaving Malicia Grim. However, there is also darkness. Death and terror lurk in the cellars, drains and tunnels. Do Maurice, Keith and the rats survive? With no simple happy ending, the reader must decide if the characters' struggles are worth enduring and their ambitions are realised.

About the author

Terry Pratchett was born in Beaconsfield, Buckinghamshire, England in 1948. He had his first story, *Business Rivals*, printed in the school magazine when he was 13. The story was published as *The Hades Business* in 1963 and he used the fee of £14 to buy a typewriter. Pratchett left school at 17 to work on a local newspaper. Part of his job was to write a weekly story column for children. As a newspaper reporter, he interviewed a local publisher, Peter Bander van Duren, and told him about a book he was working on, based on one of his children's column stories. Pratchett's manuscript was passed to the co-publishing director, Colin Smythe. Smythe liked what he read, and went on to become Pratchett's friend, publisher and later agent. The manuscript was published as Terry Pratchett's first novel, *The Carpet People*, in 1971. The first Discworld novel, *The Colour of Magic*, was published in 1983. Pratchett went on to achieve global success with his bestselling Discworld series. His extensive output won him multiple prizes, honorary degrees and a knighthood for services to literature. Terry Pratchett died in 2015.

Key facts

The Amazing Maurice and His Educated Rodents

Author: Terry Pratchett

First published: 2001 by Doubleday

Awards: In 2001, he won the Carnegie Medal for *The Amazing Maurice and His Educated Rodents*.

Did you know? This is the 28th novel in Terry Pratchett's Discworld series but the first written for children. Despite winning many awards, he always said that the Carnegie Medal was the one he was most proud of.

GUIDED READING

Chapter 1

Together discuss question 12 on the Guided Reading bookmark (page 12). Confirm an opening's function: to hook the reader. Comment on: talking animals, Maurice's scheming leadership, Keith's role, the unsettling intelligence of Dangerous Beans. Ask the children to answer the first part of question 1 on the bookmark. Ask: *What trick have Maurice, Keith and the rats been playing?* (Giving a town a plague of rats; ridding the town of the plague in return for money.) Point out how the animals became clever and the rats' dream of an island to establish their own civilisation. Suggest that the reader is intrigued by events and curious about Maurice's promise to make this last trick 'one to remember'. Assess the chapter's success. Is Maurice's promise to leave the townsfolk 'amazed' a final hook?

Chapter 2

Ask: *Do you understand the plan?* Point out the name of the town, Bad Blintz, and refer the children to Keith's book in Chapter 1. Comment on Maurice's perceptiveness as he notices: few market goods, poor people, rich buildings, a high price for a rat's tail. Why does Maurice suggest that the town rats have 'very strange tails'? (The rat-catchers' handfuls looked 'like black string'.) Suggest that the children re-read the last five pages of the chapter. Discuss and compare Maurice's and Keith's attitudes to the town. Do they both want to stay? Ask the children to discuss question 6 on the Guided Reading bookmark.

Chapter 3

Indicate the chapter heading. Refer the children to the headings for Chapters 1 and 2, also extracts from *'Mr Bunnsy Has An Adventure'*. Together discuss question 3 on the Guided Reading bookmark. Point out that lighting a candle is a new habit for the rats. Compare Hamnpork's attitude to darkness to that of the younger rats. Comment on further evidence of Dangerous Beans's intelligence: his explanation of a fear of shadows, his use of writing, his thoughts. Why does Hamnpork frequently remind the others that he is the leader? Ask the children to discuss question 3 on the Guided Reading bookmark. Investigate the behaviour and appearance of Darktan. Why does he wear belts? Why do other rats listen to him? What does he think of humans? (They are 'mad' and 'bad'.) Share answers to question 7 and the second part of question 1 on the bookmark. Point out references to *the Book* that the rats consult. What is it called? (*'Mr Bunnsy Has An Adventure'*)

Chapter 4

Read aloud the extract from *'Mr Bunnsy Has An Adventure'*. Together discuss question 3 on the Guided Reading bookmark. Ask: *How has the setting changed from the end of Chapter 3?* (It has moved from underground to above ground.) *Which story point does the plot return to?* (the end of Chapter 2) Discuss details about the town and its rat problem. What is strange about Malicia? Indicate her remarks such as 'That's not how it should go' and 'And she had big warts, I'm sure'. What does Malicia seem to expect to happen? (Real events will match stories she reads.) Point out further information about the fake rats' tails. What are the aiglets Maurice spotted? Return to your discussion of question 3 on the bookmark. Ask: *How were your predictions correct?* Comment on the kitchen setting and the frequent references to food.

Chapter 5

Direct the children to question 11 on the Guided Reading bookmark. Ask them to identify setting changes as they read the chapter. Comment on Darktan's knowledge, skills and control of others. Ask: *What are his teaching methods?* (instruction, repetition and sarcasm) Point out the philosophical discussion on what happens after death, particularly

GUIDED READING

to their 'invisible part'. Do they believe in the Bone Rat and the Big Rat Underground? Ask: *How does Maurice decide to kill the mouse?* (It cannot speak.) *What worries Darktan about the keekees in this area?* (There are no living ones.) Together discuss question 8 on the bookmark. Point out Darktan's worry about panic. What would be the result? (The Changelings would behave as rats, and run into any tunnel.) Emphasise Darktan's statement: 'this is war'. He has recognised that humans are using methods that the Changelings have never faced before. Ask the children to focus on Darktan as they discuss question 9 on the bookmark.

Chapter 6

Read the early pages of the chapter, set above ground. Together identify Malicia's story references and discuss together question 10 on the Guided Reading bookmark. Point out her reference to 'A silly one for children. Full of animals dressed as humans'. Is this book '*Mr Bunnsy Has An Adventure*'? Read the rest of the chapter. Comment on the setting change to directly below Maurice. Remind the children that Dangerous Beans is very clever. Ask: *What is surprising about the way Dangerous Beans treats the living keekee?* (He treats her as an equal.) *Why does he do this?* Suggest that he knows that living touch and smell are supplying information. *What do they do with her?* (They let her stay.) Point out the thoughts of Peaches as Darktan and Hamnpork disagree: 'This is the showdown. This is where we find out who is leader.' Ask the children to discuss question 4 on the bookmark.

Chapter 7

Together discuss question 10 on the Guided Reading bookmark, pointing out Malicia's reaction to the trapdoor and her reference to *an adventure*. Ask: *Why is the food discovery so important?* Remind the children of the town's food scarcity. Comment on Peaches's faith in '*Mr Bunnsy Has An Adventure*', carrying it with her. Ask: *What has happened to the behaviour of some educated rats?* Direct the children to question 8 on the bookmark for discussion. Read aloud the description of the caged rats. Ask: *Which senses are appealed to?* (sight, smell and hearing) Where do the two parts of the plot meet? (in the cellar) Examine Hamnpork's behaviour. Ask: *Are his emotions controlling his mind?* Investigate Maurice's behaviour as he looks after his own safety and seeks escape. Let the children discuss question 2 on the bookmark. Ask: *Who is talking to Maurice in the final pages of the chapter?* (his memory) *Which unknown rats does he smell?*

Chapter 8

Discuss how Maurice reunites with the rats and the trust Dangerous Beans shows in him. Ask: *Is Maurice worthy of this? How does Darktan differ?* (He recognises the truth about Maurice.) Investigate the despair of Dangerous Beans. How does Maurice react to Dangerous Beans's new state? (with sympathy) Together discuss question 2 on the Guided Reading bookmark. Examine Maurice's confession about eating Additives. Ask: *Why does he confess?* Examine the conversation between Malicia and Keith. Point out Keith's loyal defence of the rats and their name choices. How is Hamnpork rescued? Is it surprising that the cautious, skilful Darktan is probably in a trap? Use question 6 on the bookmark for discussion.

Chapter 9

Investigate in detail the attitudes that Dangerous Beans and Peaches's have to the book, *Mr Bunnsy Has An Adventure*. Comment on Keith's kindness as he worries about Malicia's dismissal of 'stupid stuff for ickle kids' being overheard. Point out Maurice's decision to leave town and abandon the rats. Ask: *What makes him stay?* (Maurice's new conscience and Keith.) Ask the children to focus on Keith as they discuss question 6 on the Guided Reading bookmark. Consider Darktan's state as he wonders about the Big Rat. Does this mean Darktan

GUIDED READING

is close to death? Point out the opinion that after his rescue, Darktan was different: 'his thoughts had slowed down, but got bigger'. Point out his new appreciation of the rats' need for the intelligent words and thoughts of Dangerous Beans. Comment that Darktan realises the danger of behaving like 'rats in a barrel'. Ask: *Is this new wisdom behind his decision not to start a fire?* Together discuss question 12 on the bookmark.

Chapter 10

Use question 2 on the Guided Reading bookmark to discuss Maurice's debate with his conscience. Comment on the dying Hamnpork's wish for darkness and Darktan's sympathetic compliance. Ask: *How is Hamnpork shown special respect?* (He is buried, not eaten.) Is the combination of new written language and old 'widdling' fitting for Hamnpork's grave? Point out Darktan's new understanding of leadership's burden: 'everyone waited to see what you said'. Ask: *Why does Sardines encourage him?* (Rumours that Darktan 'could stare down the Bone Rat' and his handling of Hamnpork's death.) *What important idea has Darktan had?* (War between humans and rats should end.) Together discuss question 9 on the Guided Reading bookmark, examining the debate between Dangerous Beans and Peaches about '*Mr Bunnsy*'. Investigate Darktan's speech as he leads the rats. Ask: *Which words and actions are important as he inspires the Clan for battle? What is their Dark Wood?* (the tunnels) Consider Dangerous Beans as he struggles to stay free from the trap of the Spider's enticing voice. Draw attention to Dangerous Beans's brave words: 'I am more than just a rat'. Suggest that the children discuss question 12 on the bookmark.

Chapter 11

Are the children surprised that Maurice appears in the story again? Has he changed? Point out Pratchett's use of 'it'. This implies that the cat has become a creature controlled by instinct not thinking. Ask: *What saves Dangerous Beans from the cat?* (The tiny bit that was still Maurice.) Ask: *Why does Maurice see the Grim Squeaker?* (Maurice has died, so he must lose a life.) *Why does he offer two lives? Is it to save Dangerous Beans?* Comment on Darktan's confident orders. How does Darktan react when other rats question his authority? When else does Darktan lead? (He negotiates with the mayor.) Ask the children to discuss question 4 on the bookmark.

Chapter 12

Together discuss question 6 on the Guided Reading bookmark as Maurice mediates between rats and humans. Point out Darktan's contempt for being considered 'pets'. Ask: *What is Dangerous Beans's idea?* (To appeal to the common bond between intelligent species.) Let the children discuss the second part of question 1 on the bookmark. Ask: *What happens to the dream of an island?* (This town is the best place they will find.) *What do they feel about 'Mr Bunnsy Has An Adventure'?* (It is probably 'just a pretty story'.) Examine the conversation between the mayor and Darktan. Point out Darktan's appreciation of a 'normal' life and his conclusion: this arrangement must be 'worth a try'. Ask: *What does Darktan try to learn?* (How the mayor copes with leadership.) Comment on the friendly, equal discussion between man and rat. Ask: *Why does Maurice reject a comfortable life here?* (There would be no challenge.) *What is Maurice's act of generosity?* (He gives the money to the rats.) *Is it surprising?* Ask the children to discuss questions 2 and 12 on the bookmark.

SCHOLASTIC READ & RESPOND
Bringing the best books to life in the classroom

The Amazing Maurice and His Educated Rodents
by Terry Pratchett

Focus on… Meaning

1. What has made Maurice and the talking rats so clever? Do they feel equal to or better than humans? Quote evidence.

2. Does Terry Pratchett want the reader to like or dislike Maurice? Explain why you say this.

3. What predictions can you make about what may happen in this chapter from its opening quote from *Mr Bunnsy Has An Adventure*?

4. Is the leader's position safe? Do the other rats look up to him? Supply evidence to support your answers.

Focus on… Organisation

5. Do you think the author uses setting effectively? Give an example and explain how it adds to the story.

6. How does the author build up atmosphere and information about the characters in this chapter?

Focus on… Language and features

7. Identify two or three unusual words used in rat language. Think of replacement words in human language.

8. What are the differences between unchanged rats and changed rats? Give an example of the behaviour of both in the story.

Focus on… Purpose, viewpoints and effects

9. Whose viewpoint are you aware of here? Which character(s) does the author want you to agree with? Explain your answer.

10. Do you think Malicia understands what is happening or is she imagining something else? Give examples to support your opinion.

11. Are the scenes in this chapter taking place underground or above ground? Can you find an example of both?

12. What is the author's aim in this part of the book? How does the author achieve this?

SHARED READING

Extract 1

- In this extract from Chapter 2, the kid (Keith) and Maurice, new arrivals to Bad Blintz, talk after meeting rat-catchers. Maurice's cunning, observation and self-preservation become evident.

- Invite the children to count the paragraphs. Ask: *Why are there so many?* (The text is mainly dialogue.) Point out that the speaker's name is often omitted because a new paragraph makes it obvious who is talking.

- Circle 'did' in paragraph three. Comment on the italic font. Ask: *Why is it used?* (for emphasis) *What does it suggest about the speaker?* (Keith is less observant.)

- Circle 'opportunities' in paragraph nine and 'ordinary' in the final paragraph. Invite individuals to read the paragraphs aloud, emphasising these words. Ask: *Is italic font helpful? Does it add atmosphere and information?*

- Indicate this sentence: ''What's odd about the rats?' said the kid.' Ask the children to identify spoken and non-spoken words. Circle speech marks, explaining that authors sometimes use single inverted commas rather than double. Circle the question mark. Ask: *What is its function?* (to divide the spoken and non-spoken parts of the sentence) *Which punctuation mark divides the next sentence?* Circle the comma after 'tails'.

- Direct the children to paragraph 13. Underline 'who generally told people what they wanted to hear'. What do the children infer? (Maurice may not have such a high opinion of the rats' intelligence.)

- Underline the punctuation mark completing the final sentence. Ask: *What is it?* (an ellipsis) *Why is it chosen instead of a full stop?* (It implies that Maurice wants to say more.)

Extract 2

- In this extract from Chapter 6, the prisoner rat is fed while the Changelings talk.

- Circle 'engulfing' and read the sentence aloud. Ask: *What vivid image does the verb create?* (The reader 'sees' the small rat grabbing as much food as she can.)

- Read paragraph three aloud. Underline 'Couldn't see the point of it'. Ask: *Which pronoun has been omitted from the beginning of the sentence?* (I) *Why?* Suggest that the speech sounds more natural without it.

- Question the children about their underlined sentence in paragraph three. Ask: *What does Hamnpork not understand?* (The point of capturing and then releasing him.) *What does he probably think the woman should have done?* (She should have killed him.)

- Circle 'widdled' in paragraph five. Suggest that this action demonstrates Hamnpork's instinctive feeling that rats and humans should behave as they have always done.

- Read paragraph ten aloud. Ask: *What sense does Hamnpork rely on?* (smell) Underline the paragraph's final sentence. *What does he sound dismissive of?* (thinking, writing)

- Circle the words written in italic font: 'part', 'see', 'smell', 'kind', 'lots'. Invite individuals to read the relevant sentences aloud. Ask: *How does the speaker react to the change in font?* (He uses emphasis or changes his tone.) *Is comprehension helped? Is italic font effective? Does the author use the device too frequently?*

- Investigate the final paragraph. Circle the four uses of an ellipsis. Why has the author used this punctuation mark? What does it suggest about Darktan? (He is pausing, thinking carefully about what he says.)

SHARED READING

Extract 3

- Taken from Chapter 12, this extract covers a private meeting between Darktan and the mayor.

- Circle 'it' in paragraph one. Ask: *What does 'it' refer to?* (Maurice and the senior rats' proposal for peace between humans and the Changeling rats)

- Underline 'brightened up' in paragraph two. Ask: *What does this suggest about the mayor's feelings?* (He is unsure that peace will happen.) *What has worried him?* Circle 'arguing'.

- Circle 'arguing' again in paragraph three. Ask: *How do the two characters view arguing differently?* (The mayor thinks it is a negative sign. Darktan sees it as positive.)

- Read paragraph three aloud. Underline 'I think it might work' and the paragraph's final sentence. Ask: *What do the underlined words reveal about Darktan's attitude to the proposed peace?* (He also has doubts.) Indicate the second sentence. Ask: *What does Darktan do here?* (He makes a powerful case for peace by arguing a benefit for each side.)

- Read paragraph six aloud. Ask: *What is puzzling the mayor?* (The rats spared the humans.) Circle 'advanced'. *What does its use show?* (The mayor respects the rats.)

- Investigate paragraphs eight and nine. Underline 'we just do not hate you enough' and circle 'friends'. Suggest that italic font emphasises Darktan's horror at the idea of liking humans.

- Circle 'normal', used three times in the final two paragraphs. Ask: *Why does Darktan emphasise normal to himself?* (Rats and humans all want this.)

- Underline the final paragraph. Ask: *Why is this paragraph important?* (Darktan reaches a decision: 'It must be worth a try.')

Extract 4

- This extract about rats, provides information about possible rat kings.

- Highlight the title. Explain that it indicates what the text is about.

- Underline and read aloud the opening statement. Ask: *What does it achieve?* (It introduces the subject.) Read aloud the next two sentences and discuss the first paragraph's function. Point out that having introduced the topic of rat kings, the paragraph then answers the questions 'Where?' and 'When?'.

- Question the children about divisions in the remaining text (paragraphs). Underline the bold words before paragraphs two to five. Explain that such sub-headings are common in information text. Ask: *What is their purpose?* (They help the reader to access information.)

- Circle dates and places, for example: '1564', 'Estonia', 'Mauritanum Altenburg', 'Germany', 'Otago Museum'. Emphasise that they identify times and name real places, essential in a text giving historical information.

- Circle 'mummified'. Ask: *What does it mean?* (preserved in a dried-up state) The correct term gives technical authenticity to the text.

- Read paragraph two aloud. Refer to Chapter 10 of the novel and Keith's belief that the rat-catchers have made this rat king. Suggest that Pratchett knew theories about rat kings.

- Underline 'are reported' in the first paragraph and 'have attracted' in the final paragraph. Identify each as a passive verb: a verb in which the person or thing receiving the action is the subject of the sentence. Circle and identify 'discoveries' as the subject of the first passive verb, and 'rat kings' as the subject of the last.

SHARED READING

Extract 1

Chapter 2

'I haven't seen rat-catchers like them before,' said the kid. 'They looked *nasty*. Like they enjoyed it.'

'I haven't seen rat-catchers who've been so busy but still have nice clean boots,' said Maurice.

'Yes, they *did*, didn't they...' said the kid.

'But even that's not as odd as the rats around here,' said Maurice, in the same quiet voice, as though he was adding up money.

'What's odd about the rats?' said the kid.

'Some of them have very strange tails,' said Maurice.

The kid looked around the square. The queue for bread was still quite long, and it made him nervous. But so did the steam. Little bursts of it puffed up from gratings and manhole-covers all over the place, as if the whole town had been built on a kettle. Also, he had the distinct feeling that someone was watching him.

'I think we ought to find the rats and move on,' he said.

'No, this smells like a town with *opportunities*,' said Maurice. 'Something's going on, and when something's going on, that means someone's getting rich, and when someone's getting rich, I don't see why that shouldn't be m— us.'

'Yes, but we don't want those people killing Dangerous Beans and the rest of them!'

'They won't get caught,' said Maurice. 'Those men wouldn't win any prizes for thinking. Even Hamnpork could run rings round 'em, I'd say. And Dangerous Beans has got brains corning out of his ears.'

'I hope not!'

'Nah, nah,' said Maurice, who generally told people what they wanted to hear, 'I mean our rats can out-think most humans, OK? Remember back in Scrote when Sardines got in that kettle and blew a raspberry at the old woman when she lifted the lid? Hah, even *ordinary* rats can out-think humans. Humans think that just because they're bigger, they're better— Hold on, I'll shut up, someone's watching us…'

SHARED READING

Extract 2

Chapter 6

The new rat certainly wasn't giving any trouble. For one thing, it was surrounded by rats who were big and well-fed and tough, so its body was respectfully saying *sir* as hard as it could. The Changelings had also given it some food, which it was engulfing rather than eating.

'She was in a box,' said Darktan, who was drawing on the floor with a stick. 'There's a lot of them here.'

'I got caught in one once,' said Hamnpork. 'Then a female human came along and tipped me out over the garden wall. Couldn't see the point of it.'

'I believe some humans do it to be kind,' said Peaches. 'They get the rat out of the house without killing them.'

'Didn't do her any good, anyway,' said Hamnpork, with satisfaction. 'I went back next night and widdled on the cheese.'

'I don't think anyone is trying to be kind here,' said Darktan. 'There was another rat in there with her. At least,' he added, 'there was *part* of a rat in there with her. I think she'd been eating it to stay alive.'

'Very sensible,' nodded Hamnpork.

'We found something else,' Darktan said, still drawing furrows in the dirt. 'Can you see these, sir?'

He'd drawn lines and squiggles on the floor.

'Hrumph. I can *see* them, but I don't have to know what they are,' said Hamnpork. He rubbed his nose. 'I've never needed any more than this.'

Darktan gave a patient sigh. 'Then *smell*, sir, that this is a ... a picture of all the tunnels we've explored today. It's ... the shape I have in my head. We've explored a lot of the town. There's a lot of the ...' he glanced at Peaches, 'a lot of the *kind* traps, mostly empty. There's poison all over the place. It's mostly quite old. Lots of empty live traps. Lots of killer traps, still set. And no live rats. None at all, except for our ... new friend. We know there's something very odd. I sniffed around a bit near where I found her, and I smelled rats. Lots of rats. I mean *lots*.'

Extract 3

Chapter 12

'Look,' he said, 'I think it might work, if that's what you want to ask me.'

The mayor brightened up. 'You do?' he said. 'There's a lot of arguing.'

'That's why I think it might work,' said Darktan. 'Men and rats arguing. You're not poisoning our cheese, and we're not widdling in your jam. It's not going to be easy, but it's a start.'

'But there's something I have to know,' said the mayor.

'Yes?'

'You *could* have poisoned our wells. You *could* have set fire to our houses. My daughter tells me you are very ... advanced. You don't owe us anything. Why didn't you?'

'What for? What would we have done afterwards?' said Darktan. 'Gone to another town? Gone through all this again? Would killing you have made anything *better* for us? Sooner or later we'd have to talk to humans. It might as well be you.'

'I'm glad you like us!' said the mayor.

Darktan opened his mouth to say: Like you? No, we just don't hate you enough. We're not *friends*.

But ...

There would be no more rat pits. No more traps, no more poisons. True, he was going to have to explain to the Clan what a policeman was, and why rat watchmen might chase rats who broke the new Rules. They weren't going to like that. They weren't going to like that *at all*. Even a rat with the marks of the Bone Rat's teeth on him was going to have difficulty with that. But as Maurice had said: they'll do this, you'll do that. No one will lose very much and everyone will gain a lot. The town will prosper, everyone's children will grow up, and suddenly, it'll all be *normal*.

And everyone likes things to be *normal*. They don't like to see normal things changed. It must be worth a try, thought Darktan.

SHARED READING

Extract 4

The rat king
Discoveries are reported of so-called 'rat kings'. The claims are global and span hundreds of years. However, the possibility is not widely accepted by scientists and biologists.

What is a rat king?
A rat king is said to be a number of rats joined at their tails. The tails may be intertwined because of cramped, filthy living conditions. It has been suggested that a rat king formed from a large number of rats has been created when the tails have been tied together deliberately.

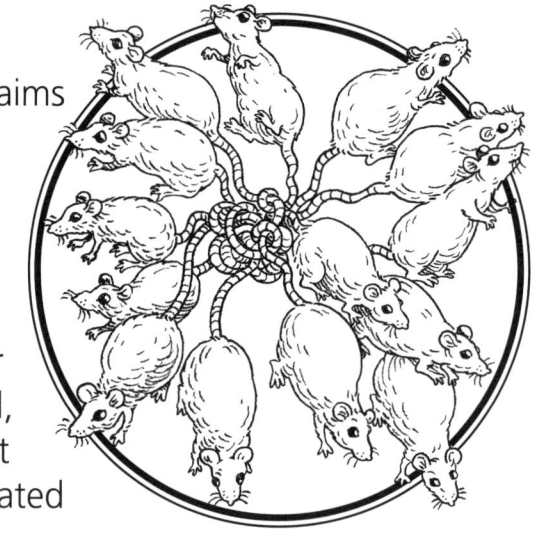

Discoveries
The earliest report of a rat king was made in 1564. The most recent claim was made in Estonia in 2005. Most of the reports have come from Germany. The science museum, Mauritianum Altenburg, displays the largest mummified rat king, consisting of 32 rats. It was supposedly found in 1828 in a miller's fireplace and smaller, preserved rat kings are displayed in other museums in Germany. A rat king found in 1930, in New Zealand, is displayed in the Otago Museum in Dunedin. In 1963, a farmer in Holland discovered a rat king made up of seven rats. X-ray images revealed callus formations at break points in the tails. Some regard the callus formations as evidence that the rats lived for a considerable period with their tails intertwined. The museum displays may be genuine, but some experts argue that they could be fakes.

The name
The name has a German origin, *Rattenkonig*. This translates as 'rat king' in English. It is thought by scholars that people may have believed that the rat king was a single rat with many bodies. 'King' referred to its total size and weight.

Superstitions
Rat kings have attracted superstitions. In the past, they were considered a bad omen, bringing misfortune, disease, plague and death. Today's novelists still use them to signify danger and malice.

GRAMMAR, PUNCTUATION & SPELLING

1. Marking boundaries

Objective
To use semi-colons, colons or dashes to mark boundaries between independent clauses.

What you need
Copies of *The Amazing Maurice and His Educated Rodents*, interactive activity 'Marking boundaries', printable page 'Marking boundaries'.

What to do
- Complete this activity after reading Chapter 5.
- Dictate this (unseen) for the children to write: 'These rats had educated skills they even surprised Maurice sometimes.'
- Let the children hold up their work, look around and compare results. Do most show two sentences? Are there alternatives?
- Write on the whiteboard:
  - a. These rats had unusual skills – they even surprised Maurice sometimes.
  - b. These rats had unusual skills; they even surprised Maurice sometimes.
- Indicate the use of one sentence. Ask: *Why can this be better?* (It keeps a link in meaning.) Identify a dash and a semi-colon, separating independent clauses. Ask: *Which mark is less formal?* (dash)
- Display this sentence: 'Maurice waited for the mouse to speak: it was silent.' Identify the colon as another means of separation. It introduces more information.
- Show the interactive activity 'Marking boundaries'. Let partners decide before you accept answers from the class. Discuss the results. Suggest that 'correct' punctuation often depends on writer preference.
- Give out copies of printable page 'Marking boundaries'. Explain that the children must decide where and how to divide the sentences into two independent clauses.

Differentiation
Support: Offer adult support in making the choices. Revise the differences between punctuation marks.

2. Passive verbs

Objective
To use passive verbs to affect the presentation of information in a sentence.

What you need
Copies of *The Amazing Maurice and His Educated Rodents*, interactive activity 'Passive verbs', photocopiable page 22 'Passive verbs', Extract 4 (Extension only).

What to do
- Use this activity at any point in the book.
- Write this sentence on the whiteboard: 'Pratchett wrote this book'. Ask: *Which word is the verb?* (wrote) *Which subject word does the action?* (Pratchett) Identify 'wrote' as an active verb.
- Write this sentence: 'This book was written by Pratchett.' Ask: *Which two words form the verb?* (was written) Point out that the subject, 'This book', has the action of the verb done to it. Hence, the verb is passive.
- Show the children the interactive activity 'Passive verbs'. Explain that all the sentences have active verbs. Give partners time to share answers as they work out the passive form so that the subject of the new sentence has the action done to it.
- Work through the interactive activity together, choosing one pair at a time to answer. Offer the answer for class discussion. Does the class agree?
- Give out copies of photocopiable page 22 'Passive verbs'. Explain that the children must rewrite the sentences so that they use passive verbs.

Differentiation
Support: Put the children into pairs and identify the starting words for the new sentence.
Extension: Ask the children to identify six passive verbs in Extract 4 on page 18.

GRAMMAR, PUNCTUATION & SPELLING

3. Silent letters

Objective
To spell some words with 'silent' letters.

What you need
Copies of *The Amazing Maurice and His Educated Rodents*, interactive activity 'Silent letters', photocopiable page 23 'Silent letters'.

What to do

- Complete this activity after reading Chapter 5.

- Remind the children of the description of a poisoned rat found in a tunnel: 'It was whimpering'. Write 'whimpering' on the whiteboard and read it aloud. Which letter in 'whimpering' do the children see but not hear? ('h' is silent) Share other words containing a silent 'h' (such as rhubarb, whine, rhyme).

- Show the children the interactive activity 'Silent letters'. Put the children into small groups. Explain that for each gap they must choose the correct word from the drop-down list.

- Work through the interactive together, choosing one group at a time to select the word for the gap. Offer the answer for class discussion. Does the class agree with the suggested answer?

- Display the text on screen 2. Ask: *Which letter is silent in each answer?*

- Put the children into pairs, each child with their own copy of photocopiable page 23 'Silent letters'. Ask the partners to take turns reading the story to each other. The listener must be on the alert for letters they cannot hear and underline those words on their text. Ask the children to circle the silent letters.

Differentiation
Support: Identify the lines of the story containing silent letters.
Extension: The children write a new story containing six words with silent letters and read it to a partner. Can the partner identify the silent letters?

4. Degrees of possibility

Objective
To use modal verbs or adverbs to indicate degrees of possibility.

What you need
Copies of *The Amazing Maurice and His Educated Rodents*, interactive activity 'Degrees of possibility', printable page 'Degrees of possibility'.

What to do

- Complete this activity after reading Chapter 8.

- Direct the children to the first sentence in Chapter 8. Ask: *What type of word is 'too'?* Confirm it as an adverb of degree. Explain that these adverbs can modify (soften) or intensify (strengthen) a verb, adjective or other adverb in the sentence.

- Show the children interactive activity 'Degrees of possibility'. Put the children into small groups. Ask them to sort the words into modifying adverbs and intensifying adverbs.

- Work through the interactive together, choosing one group at a time to place a word. Does the class agree with the suggested answer?

- Give out individual copies of the printable page 'Degrees of possibility'. Ask the children to read the text and write adverbs from the two groups that make sense in the gaps.

- Afterwards put the children into pairs, to take turns reading their version to each other. How different is the meaning?

Differentiation
Support: Read the printable sheet aloud to the children. Encourage some oral answers before they write.
Extension: Ask the children to write a diary entry by another child visiting this castle. They should try to use three modifying and three intensifying adverbs.

GRAMMAR, PUNCTUATION & SPELLING

5. Using commas

Objective
To use commas to clarify meaning or avoid ambiguity in writing.

What you need
Copies of *The Amazing Maurice and His Educated Rodents*, media resource 'Using commas', printable page 'Using commas'.

What to do
- Use this activity after reading Chapter 8.
- Direct the children to paragraph five in Chapter 8, beginning 'He cat-paddled furiously'. Ask: *Which punctuation mark is used frequently?* (a comma)
- Read the paragraph aloud as the children follow. Can they usually 'hear' the punctuation mark? Suggest that there is a link between your pauses and intonation (the rise and fall of your voice) and the placing of commas.
- Display the media resource 'Using commas'. Read the lists of facts aloud, pausing after each to discuss it and provide an example in Chapter 8 or as shown on the media resource. Point out that some writers may use a comma before *and* in a list of actions. It can be a style preference and a writer wanting to give greater clarity in a complicated list.
- Give out individual copies of printable page 'Using commas'. Suggest the children read the sentences aloud to themselves as they decide where to place the commas.

Differentiation
Support: Advise the children on the number of commas to include in each sentence. Let partners read the sentences to each other and 'listen' for commas.
Extension: Ask the children to write four sentences about the town of Bad Blintz. Each sentence must be an example of one of the rules for using commas. Challenge them to identify the rule.

6. Using suffixes

Objective
To use suffixes to convert nouns or adjectives into verbs.

What you need
Copies of *The Amazing Maurice and His Educated Rodents*, interactive activity 'Using suffixes', photocopiable page 24 'Using suffixes'.

What to do
- Complete this activity after finishing the book.
- Introduce the term 'suffix': a group of letters added to the end of a word in order to turn it into another.
- Remind the children that at one point Malicia tells Maurice 'not to criticise my proper adventure'. Write the verb 'criticise' on the whiteboard. Divide the verb into two parts: the noun 'critic' and the group of letters 'ise'. Identify 'ise' as a suffix commonly used to form verbs.
- Display interactive activity 'Using suffixes'. Explain that the children must decide whether to attach 'ise', 'ify' or 'en' to the root word. Let the children note their answers before you complete the activity together.
- Write 'notify' on the whiteboard. Explain that some root words change their spelling when a suffix is added ('note' loses 'e' before adding 'ify' to become 'notify').
- Give out individual copies of photocopiable page 24 'Using suffixes'. Suggest using lines to join the cards or pairing with them with colours. Share answers.

Differentiation
Support: Let partners work together and suggest that the children tick the verbs that they understand and consult a dictionary for the others.
Extension: Ask the children to create verbs from: 'red', 'slack', 'mobile', 'bright', 'author', 'assassin', 'fright', 'real', 'captive', 'equal', 'sad', 'intense'. Which suffixes are used?

GRAMMAR, PUNCTUATION & SPELLING

Passive verbs

- Write a new sentence, keeping the same meaning, but using a passive verb.

1. Everyone needed safe food.
_____

2. Felix made wonderful promises.
_____

3. He promised a town without rats!
_____

4. His words delighted people.
_____

5. In return, Felix demanded money.
_____

6. Felix played a cunning trick.
_____

7. He took new rats!
_____

GRAMMAR, PUNCTUATION & SPELLING

Silent letters

- Listen as your partner reads this story aloud. Underline 12 words that have a silent letter and then circle the silent letter.

Jaye's face was solemn. She wanted a proper adventure but it kept going wrong. She needed to stay calm. She knelt down to examine the new hole in the corner. Someone had cut the wood! Could a rat with extra big teeth have been gnawing?

Little did she know that two unusual mice had just been there. One had used his knife to make the cuts. Then his sword had punched the hole. For safety, his friend had written where the tunnel entrance was. There was no doubt they would find it again.

GRAMMAR, PUNCTUATION & SPELLING

Using suffixes

- Join pairs of cards, so a suffix always joins a root word to make a new verb. Be prepared for spelling changes.

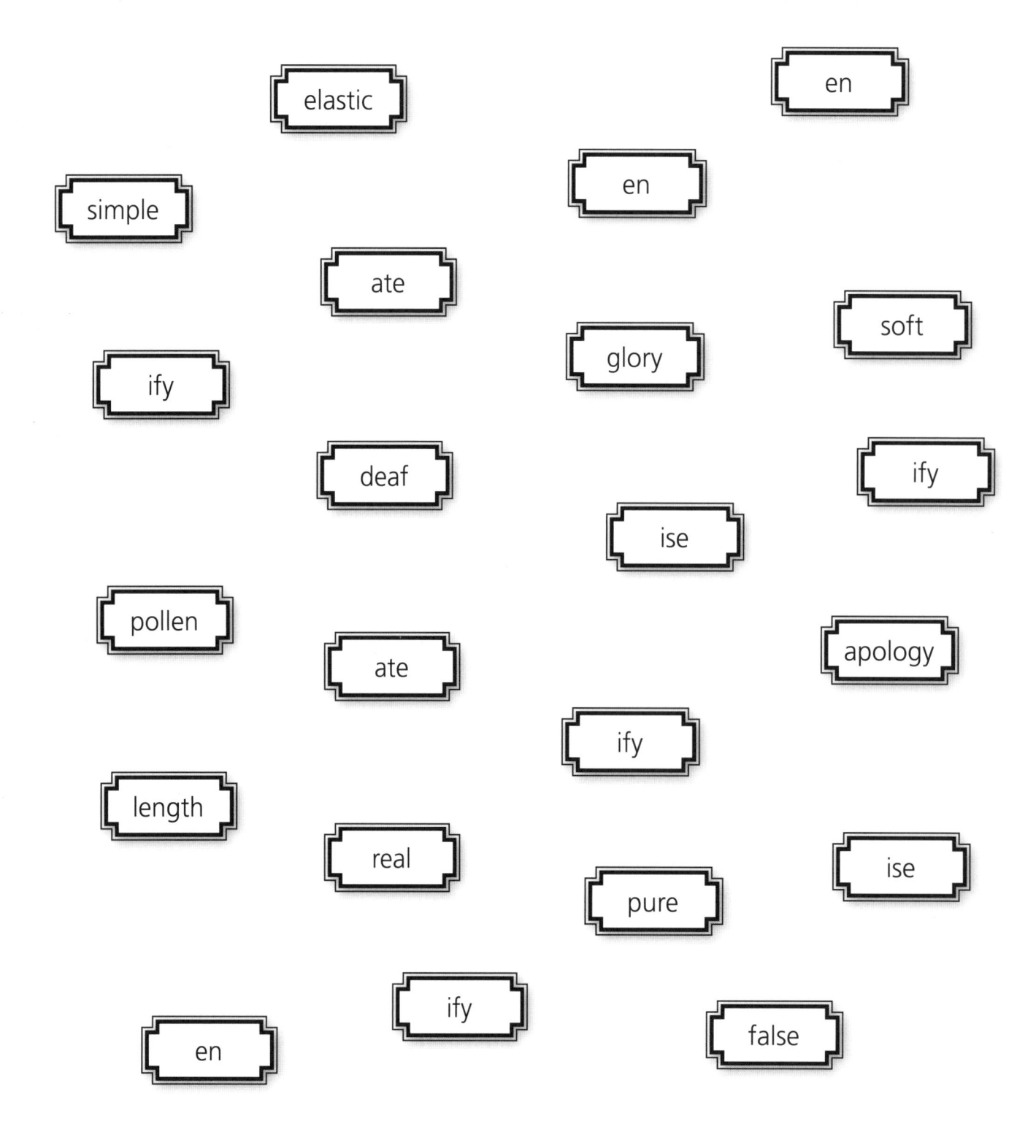

elastic	en
simple	en
	ate
	soft
ify	glory
	ify
	deaf
	ise
pollen	apology
	ate
length	ify
	real
	ise
	pure
en	ify
	false

- On the back of the sheet, list the new verbs. Write a short definition for each. Which root words needed a spelling change?

24 READ&RESPOND The Amazing Maurice and His Educated Rodents

PLOT, CHARACTER & SETTING

1. Story journal

Objective
To summarise the main ideas drawn from more than one paragraph, identifying key details that support the main idea.

What you need
Copies of *The Amazing Maurice and His Educated Rodents*, photocopiable page 29 'Story journal', internet access to paintings and music (optional).

Cross-curricular link
Art and design

What to do
- Use this activity after reading Chapter 1.
- Advise the children that this long story may be complicated. Suggest using a journal to keep track of the plot and to stay interested.
- Hold partner discussions, then class discussions about information to include: events since the last journal entry, character development, points of interest, setting, unusual language, personal response, predictions.
- Propose regular journal entries, for example, after each chapter. Advise following a format, so that chapters of character development or plot development are obvious.
- Display the headings from photocopiable page 29 'Story journal'. Organise paired, then class, discussion relating Chapter 1 to each heading. Encourage personal reactions to the book.
- For the final section, talk about varied media forms. The children may express their response to the chapter with an illustration or poster, or may use a well-known painting or piece of music.
- Give everyone photocopiable page 29 'Story journal' and an exercise book. Suggest using a double-page spread each time, using the photocopiable sheet as a template for future entries.

2. Finding answers

Objective
To predict what might happen from details stated and implied.

What you need
Copies of *The Amazing Maurice and His Educated Rodents*, photocopiable page 30 'Finding answers'.

What to do
- Complete this activity after reading Chapter 2. When posing the questions suggested here, encourage partner discussion before progressing to whole-class exchanges.
- Help the children to scan the two opening chapters. Draw attention to the numerous characters. Ask: *What different groups are there?* (talking animals, non-talking animals, humans) *Which character's name do you most notice?* Suggest that Maurice may seem important because of his position in the story's title. Ask: *Who do you think will be important in the rest of the book? Which setting will matter?*
- Give out photocopiable page 30 'Finding answers'. Ask the children to fill in the 'What I know about' section, summarising what they know so far about Maurice, Dangerous Beans and the town of Bad Blintz.
- Ask: *Are some questions unanswered?* (For example, what will happen to Maurice and Keith?) Ask the children to summarise missing information.
- Invite the children to think about how the story will end. Direct them to the box at the bottom of the photocopiable sheet to write their prediction.
- Share predictions.

Differentiation
Support: Use partner discussion as a preparation for writing. Draw attention to points to focus on.
Extension: Widen the study to include Keith and Hamnpork. Suggest the children check their prediction at different points in the story, amending as the story progresses.

PLOT, CHARACTER & SETTING

3. Purposeful language

Objective
To discuss and evaluate how authors use language, considering the impact on the reader.

What you need
Copies of *The Amazing Maurice and His Educated Rodents*, printable page 'Purposeful language'.

What to do
- Complete this activity after reading Chapter 3.
- Comment on Pratchett's regular use of italic font to bring a word to the reader's attention. Give examples: Chapter 2's first sentence suggests important information will follow; Hamnpork desperately tries to convince Peaches that he is well: 'don't', 'food', 'nothing'.
- Suggest that Pratchett may have used character names to inject humour into the book. Write 'Hamnpork' on the whiteboard. Invite children to read it aloud. Ask: *What is the name short for?* (ham and pork) *How do you react to the name?*
- Point out other surprising rat names, for example: 'Dangerous Beans', 'Sardines' and 'Peaches'. Ask the children to say some to a partner. Share reactions to reading, saying and hearing them.
- Ask: *What word does 'Malicia' remind you of?* (Malice) *What impact does the name have on your attitude to her? Why? Is Pratchett presenting her as likeable?* Refer the children to the book's first page. Ask for comments on the surname 'Grim'. Refer to Grimm's fairy tales.
- Distribute printable page 'Purposeful language'. Encourage the children to re-read relevant parts before they write about the effect of Pratchett's words on them, quoting from or referring to the text.

Differentiation
Support: Encourage oral partner collaboration before writing.
Extension: Expect greater exploration of the text, supported by appropriate quotations.

4. Reading characters

Objective
To infer characters' feelings and motives from their actions in a book.

What you need
Copies of *The Amazing Maurice and His Educated Rodents*, photocopiable page 31 'Reading characters'.

What to do
- Use this activity after reading Chapter 7.
- Point out that numerous characters have now been mentioned. Which ones spring to mind? Use partner discussion for the children to name a character they find appealing. Do they dislike any characters? Why? Share views as a class.
- Let partners discuss how writers can reveal character personalities (character actions, dialogue, comments by other characters). Make a class list.
- Suggest that the author often allows readers to form their own opinion. Refer the children to where Maurice and the rats meet up, early in Chapter 8. Point out that Darktan gives Maurice 'a much more knowing look' and says: 'Depend on him to do what, though?' The reader may infer that Darktan is less gullible than Dangerous Beans and does not trust Maurice.
- Hand out photocopiable page 31 'Reading characters'. Suggest that the children concentrate on one character at a time, working with a partner and searching the text for the actions and words that allow the reader to infer characteristics. Encourage the children to make their own adjective selection.
- Finally, ask them to write four new adjectives, one for each character.

Differentiation
Support: Reduce the choice of adjectives, leaving only the most appropriate.
Extension: Ask the children to use the chosen adjectives in a full sketch of one of the characters.

PLOT, CHARACTER & SETTING

5. Exploring structures

Objective
To read books that are structured in different ways.

What you need
Copy of *Hetty Feather* by Jacqueline Wilson, copies of *The Amazing Maurice and His Educated Rodents*, interactive activity 'Exploring structures'.

What to do
- Use this activity after Chapter 8.

- Choose a suitable novel, for example, *Hetty Feather* by Jacqueline Wilson, and read aloud from the opening pages. Ask: *How does the author refer to Hetty?* (I) Agree that *Hetty Feather* is written in the first person, the author taking the part of Hetty.

- Direct the children to the opening pages of *The Amazing Maurice and His Educated Rodents*. Ask: *How does the author refer to Maurice?* ('Maurice' or 'he') Agree that the book is written in the third person, the author being outside the story and referring to all characters by name or as 'he' or 'she'.

- Consider this book's organisation. Ask: *How is the book divided?* (paragraphs and chapters) Direct the children to Chapter 5. Point out some unusually large gaps between paragraphs. Ask: *Why has Pratchett done this?* Confirm that these gaps denote a change of setting.

- Suggest that setting could have been a useful way to structure the book.

- Display interactive activity 'Exploring structures'. Let partners discuss the events given, find them in Chapter 8, and decide on their setting. Invite them to drag and drop the sentences into place.

Differentiation
Support: Support the children in finding the relevant place in Chapter 8.
Extension: Ask the children to name six events in Chapter 7 for a partner to allocate to a setting.

6. Taking the lead

Objective
To identify and discuss themes and conventions in a wide range of writing.

What you need
Copies of *The Amazing Maurice and His Educated Rodents*, printable page 'Taking the lead'.

What to do
- Do this activity after finishing the book.

- Suggest that leadership is a strong theme in this book. Investigate the hierarchy among the rats by guiding the children in scanning Chapter 3. Ask: *Who is their leader?* (Hamnpork) *Does his position matter to him?* (He rebukes Peaches with 'Are you the leader…?')

- Ask: *Is Hamnpork confident about his position? What does he fear?* (A leadership challenge from one of the others, particularly Darktan.)

- Give out individual copies of printable page 'Taking the lead'. Ask the children to write about the quality of Hamnpork's leadership. Encourage them to justify their opinion with references to the text.

- Remind the children about Hamnpork's death in Chapter 10. Ask: *Who succeeds him?* (Darktan) Direct the children to the private meeting between Darktan and the mayor in Chapter 12. Ask: *What does Darktan want to know?* (How to cope with leadership.) *What is tiring Darktan?* (The shouting, and 'everyone expects you to decide things'.) *What reassures him?* (The mayor has the same difficulties.)

- Ask the children to complete the sheet with a paragraph about how Darktan will get on as leader. They should justify their opinion with references to the text.

Differentiation
Support: Encourage partner discussions before writing. Offer help with textual references.
Extension: Expect more writing and greater understanding of the text.

PLOT, CHARACTER & SETTING

7. Tracking development

Objective
To increase their familiarity with a wide range of books.

What you need
Copies of *The Amazing Maurice and His Educated Rodents*, printable page 'Tracking development'.

What to do
- Do this activity after finishing the book.
- Help the children to scan Chapter 1. Ask: *Is Maurice's leadership evident?* Agree that Maurice plans, orders and decides. *Do the rats recognise his authority?* As evidence, refer to the end of the chapter when Dangerous Beans, warned by Peaches, halts his objection to 'widdling on stuff'.
- Scan Chapter 2 together. Point out Maurice's perceptive observation of unlikely poverty, strange rats' tails and the rat-catchers' clean boots. Comment on greed for money, deviousness (he 'generally told people what they wanted to hear') and alertness (Maurice tells Keith to stop talking 'as someone's watching us').
- Direct the children to Chapters 7 and 8. Ask: *Is Maurice's fear surprising?* Suggest that Pratchett adds new characteristics when Maurice, worried by his 'inner cat's voice', obeys his conscience and confesses to eating the rat, Additives.
- Consider the end of the book. Ask: *Why does Maurice reject a comfortable home? Does he want more excitement? Is it surprising that he gives the money to the rats?*
- Give out printable page 'Tracking development'. Ask the children to write about the development of Maurice in four chapters. They should link their writing to the book's timeline.

Differentiation
Support: Encourage partner discussion and offer guidance on chapter selection.
Extension: Expect greater exploration of the text and original ideas.

8. Asking questions

Objective
To ask questions to improve their understanding of the text.

What you need
Copies of *The Amazing Maurice and His Educated Rodents*, printable page 'Asking questions'.

What to do
- Do this activity after finishing the book. Comment that the author should leave the reader feeling satisfied.
- Suggest that Pratchett often provokes questions in the reader's mind. Guide the children through scanning Chapter 9. Ask: *What questions are in your mind by the end of the chapter?* Encourage partner discussion and share some ideas. Write one question on the whiteboard, for example, 'Will Hamnpork recover?'
- Give out printable page 'Asking questions' for the children to write down their own two questions.
- Scan Chapter 10 together. Encourage partner discussion about questions they want answered by the chapter's end. Ask the children to write down two questions. Repeat the scanning, thinking, talking and writing process for Chapters 11 and 12.
- Suggest that by the end of the book, most questions should have been answered. Ask them to write the answers, with book quotations or references. Are any questions unanswered?
- Let the children consider the whole book and unanswered questions provoked earlier, for example, 'Could the rats become ordinary again?' Direct the children to the last part of the printable page to write two or three questions they still have. Ask: *How could Terry Pratchett answer these now?* (in a sequel)

Differentiation
Support: Accept one question at each stage.
Extension: Expect more questions and specific location of answers.

PLOT, CHARACTER & SETTING

Story journal

- Use this template to write your own journal.

Date: Chapter reached:

What has happened since the last entry?

Character developments

Atmosphere and attitudes

Setting references

Special vocabulary

My current reaction to the story so far

What I think will happen next

My idea for a supporting art form for this section (Recommend a famous painting or piece of music to suit this section. Alternatively, add your own illustration on the back of this sheet.)

PLOT, CHARACTER & SETTING

Finding answers

- Fill in what you know and what you still have to learn. Then write what you think may happen in the future.

	What I know about…	What I don't know yet about…
Maurice		
Bad Blintz		
Dangerous Beans		

What I predict will happen…

PLOT, CHARACTER & SETTING

Reading characters

- Draw lines to join two appropriate adjectives to each character. Then write four adjectives of your own and join them.

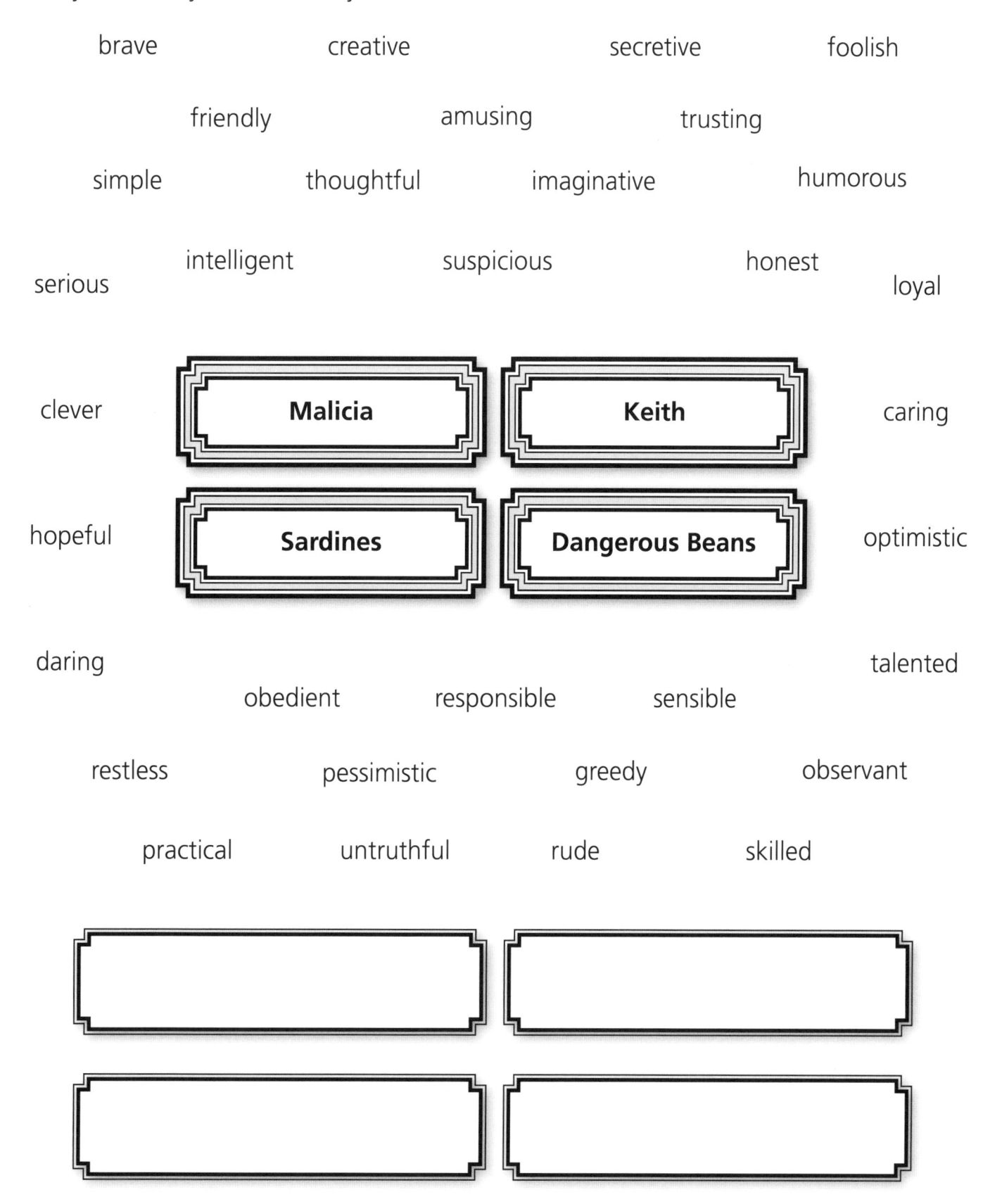

brave   creative   secretive   foolish

friendly   amusing   trusting

simple   thoughtful   imaginative   humorous

intelligent   suspicious   honest

serious   loyal

clever   **Malicia**   **Keith**   caring

hopeful   **Sardines**   **Dangerous Beans**   optimistic

daring   talented

obedient   responsible   sensible

restless   pessimistic   greedy   observant

practical   untruthful   rude   skilled

READ&RESPOND The Amazing Maurice and His Educated Rodents 31

TALK ABOUT IT

1. In the hot seat

Objective
To participate in role play.

What you need
Copies of *The Amazing Maurice and His Educated Rodents*.

What to do

- Use this activity after reading Chapter 4.

- Suggest that the reader sometimes wants more detail about characters' feelings and motives than is given explicitly in the text. For example: *How did Maurice decide on his plan? Does Keith enjoy what he is doing? How long do the rats think it will be before they reach their dream island?*

- Focus on Maurice. Invite the children, after partner discussion, to agree on and write two questions they would like to ask him. Organise the children into groups of four to compare questions. Ask them to agree on two group questions.

- Explain the term 'hot seat': role play in which a character is interviewed. Put yourself in the hot seat as Maurice. Turn away and try to make a change to your appearance (add stick-on whiskers, for example). Turn and face the class, and invite the groups to ask you their questions, making sure that you answer in role.

- Let groups discuss what they found out about Maurice's personality and motivation. Compare findings as a class.

- Select a different character: Keith, Hamnpork, Dangerous Beans, Malicia. Repeat the task as a group activity, one group member taking the hot seat to answer the others' questions.

Differentiation
Support: Provide the children with question starters.
Extension: Ask the children to make close references to the text.

2. Talk it over

Objective
To play an active part in a conversation with others about a topic.

What you need
Copies of *The Amazing Maurice and His Educated Rodents*.

What to do

- After reading Chapter 6, complete this activity in a spacious room.

- Refer to Hamnpork's complaints in Chapter 1, for example: 'If that's what thinking means, I'm glad that I don't do any.' Suggest that he finds it difficult to adapt to a Changeling's ways. He needs a guide. Set a scenario of a special meeting, with Hamnpork moving from rat to rat, talking to them about being his guide.

- Ask partners to take the roles of Hamnpork and Sardines. On your signal, they should begin their dialogue (made up as they go along) to discover if they can work together. Keep this improvisation short.

- Signal the children to stop. Ask one pair to remain in character as the other children question them about how they felt. Are they willing to work together?

- Ask partners to repeat the exercise as Hamnpork talks to Nourishing, Darktan and Peaches.

- Finally, suggest that Hamnpork has named four possible guides: Nourishing, Sardines, Darktan and Peaches. Secretly, these four meet to decide who it will be. Let the children divide into groups of four and improvise dialogue for their meeting. What does each group decide?

- Share conclusions as a class.

Differentiation
Support: Provide conversation openers.
Extension: Ask the children to use paired improvisation for humans in the story, as Malicia searches for a friend.

TALK ABOUT IT

3. Hand or mind?

Objective
To participate in discussions and debates.

What you need
Copies of *The Amazing Maurice and His Educated Rodents*, photocopiable page 35 'Hand or mind?', media resource 'Hand or mind?'.

What to do
- Complete this activity after reading Chapter 9.
- Suggest that Hamnpork may die soon. Comment that the author has been contrasting his two likely successors: Darktan and Dangerous Beans. Pratchett has emphasised Darktan's practical skills and Dangerous Beans's thoughtful intelligence. Hold a brief discussion about the two rats.
- Put the children into pairs with a copy of photocopiable page 35 'Hand or mind?'. Encourage partner and class discussion of the statements on the sheet. Point out that some statements may support either case. (For example, 'Dangerous Beans thinks carefully before making any decisions.')
- Ask partners to discuss and decide which rat to support: Darktan or Dangerous Beans. (Ensure there are children supporting both sides.) The children must choose and cut out the statements they think will support that case.
- Suggest writing notes that list around three new arguments supporting Darktan or Dangerous Beans.
- Give yourself the role of chairing the debate and listening to arguments from both sides. Allow everyone to speak.
- Finally, sum up what you have heard. Use the media resource 'Hand or mind?' and listen to the opinions. Do some children want to change their minds? Ask the children to make their final decision and vote.

Differentiation
Support: Suggest children read out the statement that they think is the most effective argument.
Extension: Ask children to argue a third way: sharing the leadership.

4. Frozen moments

Objective
To use spoken language to develop understanding through speculating, hypothesising, imagining and exploring ideas.

What you need
Copies of *The Amazing Maurice and His Educated Rodents*, photocopiable page 36 'Frozen moments'.

What to do
- Use this activity after finishing the book.
- Explain the term 'freeze-frame': the children take on the roles of story characters and create a still picture of a moment in the story.
- Guide the children in scanning Chapters 2, 3 and 4. Arrange the children in groups of four. Give each group one of the cards from photocopiable page 36 'Frozen moments'. Ask them to create a freeze-frame for that part of the story.
- Allow 5 to 10 minutes for group discussion and rehearsal. Encourage every member of the group to contribute to decision making.
- Let each group present their freeze-frame to the class. Can the class identify the story moment? Do they recognise the characters? Select individual characters to step out of the tableau and say what they are thinking.
- For other characters in the tableau, encourage the audience to consider what they may be thinking. Use thought-tracking, when an audience member stands next to that character and speaks their thoughts aloud.
- Talk about the relevance of facial expression and body language in freeze-frames. Ask the class: *Which expressions and body language helped you for thought-tracking? How?*

Differentiation
Support: The teacher moves among the groups, offering suggestions for poses.
Extension: Ask the children to plan alternative freeze-frames for different character feelings.

▼ TALK ABOUT IT

5. Telling a story

Objective
To give well-structured narratives for different purposes, including for expressing feelings.

What you need
Copies of The Amazing Maurice and His Educated Rodents, photocopiable page 37 'Telling a story'.

What to do
- Complete this activity after finishing the book.
- Comment that the final chapter covers a strange day, with discussions between humans and animals. Darktan, Maurice and the mayor will be thinking about what has happened. They probably need to talk to someone about their decision.
- Guide the children through Chapter 12. Point out the early discussion; the formal meeting; the contract; acceptance by Dangerous Beans that the Book was just a story; Darktan's and the mayor's meeting; the desire for 'normal' life. Talk about Maurice's generosity with the money; Keith's independence; Malicia's admission of loneliness; Keith and Malicia's blossoming friendship; Maurice's departure.
- Ask the children to decide which character to be: Darktan, Maurice or the mayor. As storytellers, they must organise their facts in order, describe their feelings and include details, perhaps with information known only to them.
- Give the children photocopiable page 37 'Telling a story' and ask them to make notes and sketches to remind them what happened. Emphasise that they will be telling, not reading, their story.
- Let the children practise their storytelling on partners. Organise storytelling groups, so everyone experiences speaking to a group.

Differentiation
Support: Suggest doing pictorial and one-word notes for a reduced number of cue cards.
Extension: Ask the children to take the role of Dangerous Beans, Malicia or Keith.

6. Conscience alley

Objective
To use spoken language to develop understanding through speculating, hypothesising, imagining and exploring ideas.

What you need
Copies of The Amazing Maurice and His Educated Rodents.

What to do
- Complete this activity after finishing the book.
- Direct the children to Chapter 8, when Maurice's inner voice, his conscience, makes him confess to eating Additives. Suggest that his conscience may have spoken to him again when he was leaving town.
- Divide the class into two groups: Group A represents Maurice's conscience, Group B represents his bad side. Ask Group A to think of comments to persuade Maurice to leave the money to the rats. Ask Group B to think of comments to encourage him to take the money.
- Organise the two groups into parallel lines facing each other. Take the role of Maurice and walk down the 'alley' between the lines. As you reach children, nod to them to speak their comments. At the end of the alley, having listened to their voices, make your decision.
- Choose children to act as Maurice and repeat the conscience alley. Does each Maurice reach the same decision?
- Try the activity with other situations from the book, for example: Maurice finds the mouse in Chapter 5. Create smaller conscience alleys so that more children experience listening to their conscience.

Differentiation
Support: Provide sample comments and let children speak with a partner in the conscience alley activity.
Extension: Ask children to plan a conscience alley situation for a rat-catcher or Malicia.

TALK ABOUT IT

Hand or mind?

- Cut out all the statements. Do you want Darktan or Dangerous Beans to be the next leader? Choose the statements which support your case.

Darktan is a rat of action, who believes too much thinking can be troublesome.

Dangerous Beans is very intelligent and is guided by the *Mr Bunnsy* book.

Dangerous Beans thinks carefully before making any decisions.

Darktan wears a belt of tools and weapons, ready for any emergency.

Dangerous Beans has strong ethical principles and disapproves of eating rats.

Darktan can deal with different traps, and teach others.

TALK ABOUT IT

Frozen moments

- Cut out the cards.

In the mayor's kitchen in Chapter 4, Malicia displays empty cupboards and grumbles. Behind her, Sardines abseils down from the ceiling. Maurice pulls faces at Sardines to try to make him go away.
In town in Chapter 2, Keith starts to pick up a tangle of tails. Two unpleasant-looking rat-catchers are nearby. One rat-catcher's boot holds the tails down. Maurice stares inquisitively at the tails.
In Chapter 3, deep underground, Darktan gives instructions to the platoons of rats. Sardines and Nourishing listen carefully. Hamnpork sits apart, looking tired and annoyed.
In Chapter 5, in a tunnel, Darktan examines a trap with cheese in it. Sardines holds a candle to give him light. Darktan holds a piece of wood with a sliver of mirror on it. Nourishing and Inbrine watch.
In Chapter 1, Maurice overlooks Bad Blintz and encourages the rats to make this trick their best. Dangerous Beans has started to object, but Peaches has made a warning sound to make him agree. Keith is holding his pipe.
In Chapter 7, Keith and Malicia lead the way into a cellar with cages of rats. Maurice stays a little way behind. Hamnpork screams at Malicia to free the rats.
In Chapter 10, in the cellar, Hamnpork lies on the floor, weak and near death. Darktan and Sardines are on either side of him. Nourishing is nearby. Sardines snuffs out the candle with his hat.
At the meeting in Chapter 12, Maurice marches up and down the table. Peaches and Mr Raufman discuss rules. Darktan sits at one end, his head drooping with tiredness.

TALK ABOUT IT ▼

Telling a story

- Write notes to complete the cards and use them to help you tell the story from the point of view of Darktan, Maurice or the mayor.

Introducing yourself
Who are you?
_____

How did you feel at the start of today?
_____

Rats talking to humans
Do the rats and humans trust each other?
_____

Why did both sides agree to talk?
_____

Important discussions
Who was your discussion with?
_____

Did you agree on anything?
_____

The new contract
Do you think it is going to work?
_____

What still worries you?
_____

When Maurice leaves town
How are you feeling now?
_____

READ&RESPOND The Amazing Maurice and His Educated Rodents

GET WRITING

1. Reducing text

Objective
To draft and write by précising longer passages.

What you need
Copies of *The Amazing Maurice and His Educated Rodents*, computers.

What to do
- Use this activity after reading Chapter 4.
- Suggest that the editor is asking for a shorter chapter. Agree that Chapter 4 could be reduced with less detail in Malicia's exaggerations about her life.
- Introduce the word 'précis': a shorter version of a text. Point out that when writers realise that their text takes up too much space, they write a précis or summary of it.
- Hold partner discussions about what a précis should include, before sharing ideas. Agree that main points need to be kept, but reworded. Unnecessary detail may be omitted. Pratchett will want to retain his style.
- Read aloud the text on the two pages in the first half of Chapter 4, when Malicia talks 'all about me'. Suggest that the editor wants Pratchett to reduce this part from about 250 words to no more than 175. Share ideas on what he will keep (for example, step-sisters) and what he may omit (for example, cupboards). Ask: *What must remain clear?* (Malicia lies or exaggerates.)
- Let the children make notes before typing a rough draft and final précis.

Differentiation
Support: Let children do a draft précis with a partner before typing their own.
Extension: Ask children to halve the length of the final two pages of Chapter 4. They should report some of what was said rather than using direct speech.

2. Choosing the form

Objective
To select the appropriate form and use other similar writing as models of their own.

What you need
Copies of *The Amazing Maurice and His Educated Rodents*, photocopiable page 41 'Simple stories'.

What to do
- Do this activity after reading Chapter 5.
- Point out that each chapter begins with an extract from '*Mr Bunnsy*'. Ask: *Is the reader just being entertained?* Suggest that it contains the theme for the chapter.
- Explain that quoting any story of this genre would work equally well, as long as the theme was suitable. Put the children into pairs to discuss an animal's name and story title. Share ideas, for example, 'Mrs Red Hen' or 'Mr Quacky'. What would their story be about? Ask the children to make a note of their decisions.
- Direct the children to Chapter 5's extract and read it aloud. Ask: *What theme is suggested?* (individual courage) Point out: simple vocabulary; human-like animal characters; babyish names; alliteration; an easy-to-follow story; traditional phrases.
- Give out individual copies of photocopiable page 41 'Simple stories'. The children must create extracts for the themes in Chapters 1, 2 and 3, using their story idea. Suggest working on one chapter 'extract' at a time, jotting down names, words or phrases and writing a rough draft of 25–40 words. Partners could read aloud to each other for reaction and suggestions for improvement. Then they should write the polished version on the sheet.

Differentiation
Support: Let partners collaborate on their writing.
Extension: Suggest children write extracts for Chapters 4 and 5 on the back of the photocopiable sheet.

GET WRITING

3. Story planning

Objective
To note and develop initial ideas.

What you need
Copies of *The Amazing Maurice and His Educated Rodents*, photocopiable page 42 'Story planning'.

What to do
- Complete this activity after finishing the book.
- Invite the class to imagine that the author is to write a sequel in keeping with the original book. Ask: *What could stay the same?* (perhaps the main character, Maurice; a simple boy companion; human-like animals; the writing style) *What could change?* (There could be new characters, a new plotline, setting, plan or problem.)
- Ask partners to share ideas for a sequel. Prompt them with questions. Ask: *Where is the story set?* (a different town) *What is the problem?* (Local ants have invaded houses.) *How does Maurice become involved?* (He has a new plan.) *Who helps him?* (Maurice contacts Darktan, Dangerous Beans and Peaches.) *What dangers are there? Are there struggles?* (They meet the Ant King.) *What is the ending?*
- Recap with the class a story's structure of chronological sections: opening, incidents, complications, events to sort them out, ending. Talk about the value of sub-plots to keep readers interested.
- Give out photocopiable page 42 'Story planning'. Invite the children to complete their plan with brief notes. Keep the plans for the next activity.

Differentiation
Support: Let partners work together on the same story. Provide ideas for one or two sections.
Extension: Encourage children to write detailed character notes on the back of the sheet.

4. Becoming authors

Objective
To describe settings, characters and atmosphere and integrate dialogue.

What you need
Copies of *The Amazing Maurice and His Educated Rodents*, the children's completed story planners from 'Story planning'.

What to do
- Remind the children of the previous activity: planning a sequel to *The Amazing Maurice and His Educated Rodents*.
- Re-read Chapter 5's early pages, which are typical of Pratchett's writing style. Emphasise that the children need to match it when writing. Point out: adverbs, atmosphere, detailed descriptions, fast-moving plot, setting, abundant and realistic dialogue, application of direct speech rules and emphasised spoken words ('easy', 'I'll', 'exactly', 'creaking'). Do they help the reader to 'hear' the speakers?
- Direct the children to Chapter 4's final paragraph. Suggest that Pratchett often finishes chapters at points of excitement, drama or danger.
- Return the children's 'Story planning' sheets from the previous activity. Let them use their notes to tell their story outline to a partner.
- Allocate time for the children to write the story, and suggest they consider a target length and add it to their notes.
- Allow the children to write their story. Once complete, suggest peer and group review.

Differentiation
Support: Encourage children to work in groups of up to five and share the writing, each developing one section or chapter.
Extension: Invite children to consider introducing humour, animal vocabulary and interesting chapter headings.

▼ GET WRITING

5. Writing a review

Objective
To select appropriate grammar and vocabulary, understanding how such choices can change and enhance meaning.

What you need
Copies of *The Amazing Maurice and His Educated Rodents*, interactive activity 'Book reviews'.

What to do
- Complete this activity after finishing the book.
- Explain that some books are published in two editions: one for adults, one for children. Use the term 'crossover books' and discuss examples by authors such as JK Rowling and Philip Pullman.
- Suggest that *The Amazing Maurice and His Educated Rodents* is a crossover novel. Ask: *What will children enjoy?* (animal characters, names, rat words, battles) *What will appeal to adults?* (mental struggles for ethical behaviour, a conscience, religious questions of creation and an afterlife)
- Comment that a book review's format varies. Read some examples or use ones from the media resource 'Book reviews'. Explain that you chose *The Amazing Maurice and His Educated Rodents* for the children after reading reviews in an educational magazine. Suggest that a magazine for adult readers would have featured reviews with different vocabulary.
- Invite the children to write a review of *The Amazing Maurice and His Educated Rodents*. They must make clear their recommendation for one reader: adult or child.

Differentiation
Support: Offer suggestions and encourage partner discussion when children decide what they most like or dislike, and the recommended reader.
Extension: Let the children use their completed page as a plan for writing a polished magazine or website review.

6. Creating an ending

Objective
To plan their writing by identifying the purpose of the writing.

What you need
Copies of *The Amazing Maurice and His Educated Rodents*, photocopiable page 43 'Creating an ending'.

What to do
- Complete this activity after finishing the book.
- Help the children to scan the final 12 pages of the book, from where the mayor and Darktan go for a private meeting. Suggest that these pages form the story's ending. Ask: *What is the function of the ending?* Compare ideas, agreeing on common features: loose ends can be tied up; plot questions may be answered; plot problems ought to be resolved.
- Identify some of these features in the ending of this book. Point out that the progress of Maurice and his plan have been followed; a place for the rats' peaceful civilization has been found; questions about Keith and the next rat leader have been answered.
- Suggest that the author could have ended the story differently. Let partners tell each other one possible change before you share some ideas as a class.
- Set the scenario. Pratchett's final pages have been lost! The children must write a new ending. Give out individual copies of photocopiable page 43 'Creating an ending' for them to make planning notes.
- Let partners discuss their completed plans before, independently, writing their own ending.

Differentiation
Support: Suggest the children draw pictures of their ending before writing the text.
Extension: Ask the children to plan and talk about a second alternative ending.

GET WRITING

Simple stories

- Write extracts from your animal book to suit these themes:
  - Chapter 1: Greedy for money
  - Chapter 2: Needing food
  - Chapter 3: Dangerous places

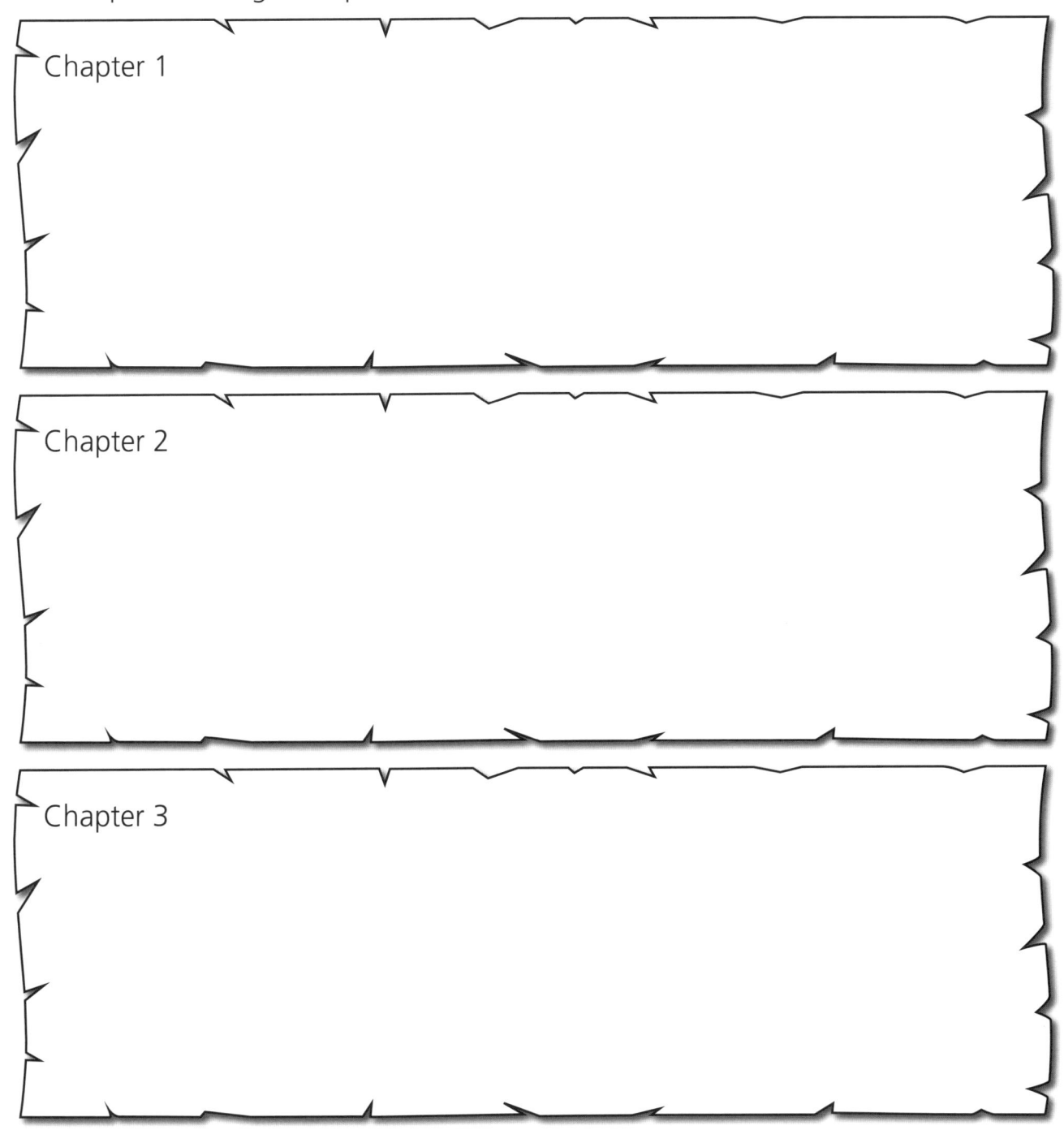

Chapter 1

Chapter 2

Chapter 3

- Write the title of your book at the bottom of this page.

From _____

ASSESSMENT

1. Using hyphens

Objective
To use hyphens to avoid ambiguity.

What you need
Copies of *The Amazing Maurice and His Educated Rodents*, interactive activity 'Using hyphens', printable page 'Using hyphens'.

What to do

- Use this activity after reading Chapter 2.

- Direct the children to the early pages of Chapter 2. Point out and write on the whiteboard: 'accordion-players' and 'stupid-looking'. Ask the children to identify the underlined punctuation mark (hyphen). Ask: *How does a hyphen differ from a dash?* Show in nearby examples in the text that it is shorter.

- Explain that a hyphen is used in various ways. One use is to join two words into one idea (for example, 'money-mad', 'never-thinking'). Another use is to avoid confusion and to make clear what word is being used (for example, 're-press' means 'to press again'; 'repress' means 'to hold things in').

- Display the interactive activity 'Using hyphens'. Put the children into pairs to decide on their answers. Invite partners to tackle a sentence. After completing the text, examine screen 2 together. Do the children find the new text easier to read and understand?

- Give out copies of the printable page 'Using hyphens' for the children to complete individually.

Differentiation

Support: Let children complete the printable sheet with a partner. Let an adult read aloud and explain the pairs of words before they write.
Extension: Invite children to identify other hyphenated words in Chapters 1 and 2. Can they think of any examples of their own?

2. Spelling homophones

Objective
To continue to distinguish between homophones and other words which are often confused.

What you need
Copies of *The Amazing Maurice and His Educated Rodents*, interactive activity 'matching homophones', printable page 'Spelling homophones'.

What to do

- Complete this activity after reading Chapter 10.

- Write on the whiteboard: 'It was like a maze of tunnels down there.' Can partners tell each other the underlined word's meaning? Share definitions, confirming 'confusing arrangement'.

- Add to the whiteboard: 'One tunnel led to a cellar containing a sack of maize.' Ask partners to share the underlined word's meaning. Confirm 'corn'. What do the children notice about the underlined words, when they are read aloud? (the same sound)

- Identify 'maze' and 'maize' as homophones. Share other homophones or words often confused. Use 'steal/steel', 'tail/tale', 'story/storey' and 'who's/whose' in oral sentences for the children to identify, define and spell.

- Display interactive activity 'Matching homophones'. Explain that the words must be matched in pairs. Let partners work together, using dictionaries to check meanings, before volunteers join the pairs. As each pair is created, ask half the class to read the words aloud. Do the listeners hear words that sound the same? What are the meanings?

- Distribute printable page 'Spelling homophones'. Encourage the children to check meanings and differences in pairs of words before using them.

Differentiation

Support: Put the children into pairs, and let an adult read aloud and explain the pairs of words before they write.
Extension: Ask children to think of 8–10 more pairs of homophones and use them correctly.

ASSESSMENT

3. Major or minor?

Objective
To draw inferences such as inferring characters' feelings, thoughts and motives from their actions, and justifying inferences with evidence.

What you need
Copies of *The Amazing Maurice and His Educated Rodents*, media resource 'Major or minor?', printable page 'Major or minor?'.

What to do
- Use this activity after finishing the book.
- Ask pairs to share what they know about Peaches. Join pairs for groups of four to exchange thoughts.
- Share ideas as a class. Comment on: Peaches's ability to read human and create a written language for the rats; official carrier of *'Mr Bunnsy'*; understanding of Hamnpork and happenings among the rats; ability to intimidate even humans with her mind.
- Suggest that Peaches may seem a minor character, but has significant influence on the others' actions and the course of the plot.
- Point out interesting details, for example: Maurice's daunted reaction to her 'Ahem' and 'odd little questions'; his failure to trick her by 'just talking fast' (Chapter 1); her influence over Dangerous Beans (Chapters 1 and 11); the information that she gives to Darktan about Hamnpork (Chapter 3); 'rather frightening some of the councillors' (Chapter 12).
- Display the media resource 'Major or minor?'. Read the screen's instruction aloud. Show each picture and allow partner discussion before the children write a paragraph independently about the influence Peaches has over the character. The children may write on the printable page 'Major or minor'.

Differentiation
Support: Accept simple explanations and limited reference to the text.
Extension: Expect more writing, greater originality and closer textual reference.

4. Sombre and serious

Objective
To note and develop initial ideas.

What you need
Copies of *The Amazing Maurice and His Educated Rodents*, printable page 'Sombre and serious'.

What to do
- Use this activity after finishing the book.
- Suggest that this book is not only a light, amusing story about animals with magical powers, but also a dark, serious book about fear, self-control and goodness.
- Direct the children to Chapter 3. Read Dangerous Beans's explanation and advice about shadows aloud. Suggest that Pratchett is commenting that everyone has inner fears.
- Read the *'Mr Bunnsy'* extract heading for Chapter 10 aloud. Direct the children to the middle of Chapter 10 where Darktan suggests that the rats are now in their 'Dark Wood'. Ask: *What is the 'something terrible'?* (an evil force) *How can their terror be overcome?* (facing up to fear and not panicking)
- Scan the few pages after Darktan's speech. Re-read the conversations with the Spider. Explain that Dangerous Beans uses mental strength to withstand the Spider's evil power.
- Direct the children to Chapter 11. Point out Maurice's question about a *Big Cat in the Sky* and the answer. Indicate and define the word *theology*. Could the author be voicing his own thoughts?
- Give out individual copies of the printable page 'Sombre and serious' for the children to discuss in pairs. Suggest making notes, before writing a preliminary draft and final piece.

Differentiation
Extension: Expect more perceptive analysis and a focus on people, not animals.

ASSESSMENT

5. Investigating words

Objective
To explore the meaning of words in context.

What you need
Copies of *The Amazing Maurice and His Educated Rodents*.

What to do

- Use this activity after finishing the book.

- Write this on the whiteboard: '"So,' said the voice of Malicia. 'You don't have a knife of any kind?"' Underline 'kind' for the children to tell a partner its meaning. Agree a replacement word or phrase to write beside the sentence, for example, 'type'.

- Write this on the whiteboard: 'Malicia complained that her dreadful step-sisters were never kind to her.' Underline 'kind' for the children to define to a partner. Share ideas and write a replacement, for example, 'friendly'.

- Ask: *Why is 'kind' defined differently?* (The context changes.) Explain that a word may change its meaning. Look at 'kind' in a dictionary. Are other meanings suggested?

- Suggest that Pratchett often gives readers an insight into characters through their language. Point out the trusting innocence of Dangerous Beans ('I believe he is a decent cat at heart.') and Peaches's observant wariness ('Ahem. That remains to be seen.')

- List these words on the whiteboard: 'craning', 'crammed', 'council', 'keen', 'allegations', 'commotion', 'muffled', 'ill-gotten', 'unhygienic', 'negotiator', 'grace', 'clients'. Identify their context as the first four pages of Chapter 12. The children must copy the phrase containing the word, underline the word and write a replacement word or phrase of the same meaning. Emphasise considering the word's context and using a dictionary well.

Differentiation
Support: Expect fewer completed definitions and accept partner support.
Extension: Let children repeat the activity with vocabulary from Chapter 9.

6. Finding a future

Objective
To identify and discuss themes and conventions across a wide range of writing.

What you need
Copies of *The Amazing Maurice and His Educated Rodents*, photocopiable page 47 'Finding a future'.

What to do

- Use this activity after finishing the book.

- Put the children into pairs. After asking questions, listen in to partner discussion. Allow time for everyone one to speak before you accept answers from the class.

- Direct the children to Chapter 1. Comment on the insistence of Peaches on the last time for 'the silly plague of rats trick'. Ask: *Does Dangerous Beans agree?* (yes) *What is his dream for the future?* (He wants to reach an island where the rats could build their own future.)

- Suggest that a better future is an important theme in this story. Ask: *What are Keith's hopes?* (avoiding danger and playing his flute) *What is Maurice's dream?* (a comfortable home and doting owner)

- Ask partners to consider how the story ends. Do characters get what they first wanted? Agree that all settle for a normal life that they think will make them happy.

- Give out individual copies of photocopiable page 47 'Finding a future' for the children to complete independently. They should draw and write about the characters' early dreams and the normal life they settle for at the end.

Differentiation
Support: Direct children to relevant text before they complete the photocopiable sheet.
Extension: Expect greater understanding and closer reference to the text.

ASSESSMENT

Finding a future

- Draw and write what these characters see as their future.

	At the beginning…	By the end…
The rats		
Maurice		
Keith		

READ&RESPOND *The Amazing Maurice and His Educated Rodents*

SCHOLASTIC

Available in this series:

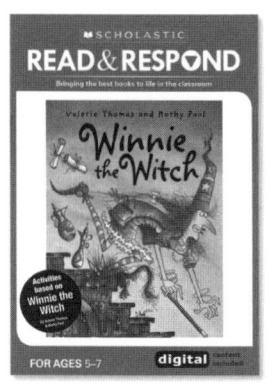

Winnie the Witch (Ages 5–7)	978-1407-16066-5	
Stick Man (Ages 5–7)	978-1407-16053-5	
Danny the Champion of the World (Ages 7–11)	978-1407-16054-2	
Diary of a Wimpy Kid (Ages 7–11)	978-1407-16055-9	
The Amazing Maurice and his Educated Rodents (Ages 7–11)	978-1407-16056-6	
Goodnight Mister Tom (Ages 7–11)	978-1407-16057-3	
Jasper's Beanstalk (Ages 5–7)	978-1407-16058-0	NOV 2016
Oliver's Vegetables (Ages 5–7)	978-1407-16059-7	NOV 2016
Bill's New Frock (Ages 7–11)	978-1407-16060-3	NOV 2016
George's Marvellous Medicine (Ages 7–11)	978-1407-16061-0	NOV 2016
Millions (Ages 7–11)	978-1407-16062-7	NOV 2016
War Horse (Ages 7–11)	978-1407-16063-4	NOV 2016
Percy Jackson and the Lightning Thief (Ages 7–11)	978-1407-16064-1	NOV 2016
Zog (Ages 5–7)	978-1407-16065-8	JAN 2017
Owl Babies (Ages 5–7)	978-1407-16052-8	JAN 2017
How to Train Your Dragon (Ages 7–11)	978-1407-16067-2	JAN 2017
Why the Whales Came (Ages 7–11)	978-1407-16068-9	JAN 2017
Varjak Paw (Ages 7–11)	978-1407-16069-6	JAN 2017
Carrie's War (Ages 7–11)	978-1407-16070-2	JAN 2017
The Boy in the Striped Pyjamas (Ages 7–11)	978-1407-16071-9	JAN 2017

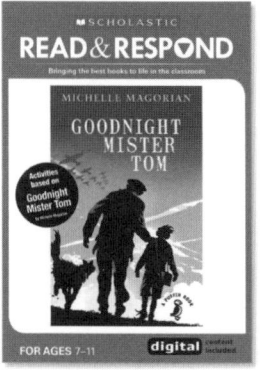

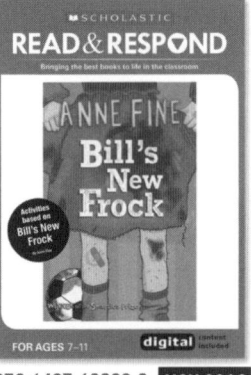

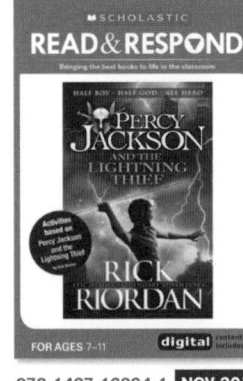

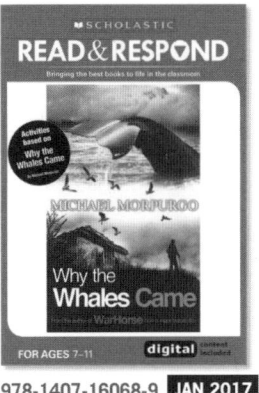

To find out more, call: 0845 6039091
or visit our website www.scholastic.co.uk/readandrespond